WORKING WITH GROUPS

Rob Long

D1418104

First published 2005 by David Fulton Publishers Ltd

This edition published 2014 by Routledge
2 Park Square, Milton Park, Abingdon, Oxon OX14 4RN
711 Third Avenue, New York, NY 10017

Routledge is an imprint of the Taylor & Francis Group, an informa business

British Library Cataloguing in Publication Data
A catalogue record for this book is available from the British Library.

ISBN 184312 371 1
ISBN 978-1-84312-371-2 (pbk)

Typeset by FiSH Books, London

Contents

1 Introduction

Kim is six years old and has one-to-one support due to her aggressive behaviour. The teaching assistant in Kim's class reports that she is a pleasure to work with and that, when she is on her own, Kim is polite and co-operative. But when she is with her peers Kim is pushy and aggressive unless she is getting her own way.

It is not uncommon for children who face emotional and behavioural difficulties to behave well in a one-to-one situation with an adult. It is when they are in a group with their peers that their behaviour deteriorates dramatically. More and more today we refer to the difficulties of such children as being *social*, emotional and behavioural, rather than just emotional and behavioural. Yet, while most of us work with children in groups, little formal training in the understanding of group dynamics is provided. The more we understand the nature, purpose and function of groups then the better equipped we will be to support children who find such skills as turn-taking and sharing difficult to master or achieve.

In this chapter we will:

- define key terms
- consider the importance of groups
- explore why groups are difficult for children with social, emotional and behavioural difficulties.

What is a group?

While there is no hard and firm definition of what constitutes a group the following features are central. A group comprises members who:

1

- relate to each other
- can influence each other
- have an identity
- communicate with each other
- have some form of hierarchy.

This leads us to the next key term:

Group dynamics

When social psychologists were beginning to study groups, a key figure was Kurt Lewin who was carrying out research in the 1930s. He emphasised that groups are dynamic in that their members influence each other. Groups give identity to members and can pressure them to conform. Since Lewin's time our understanding of group dynamics has increased significantly. In fact, to many people, all psychology is essentially group psychology as that is where we live our lives – in a range of different groups. This includes the family as well as the class in school that a child belongs to.

What purpose do groups serve for young people?

We are all social animals. When we were children we depended on our carers to survive. Our personal identity is developed through our relationship to others, both within our family and outside. For example, I am a husband to a wife, a father to children, a son to a mother, a colleague at work. We are never without any links to one or other group.

As human beings we have many needs. We all need food, shelter and warmth. But after these basic needs are met other needs emerge that relate to social groups. Groups provide us with the following three core human needs:

1   The need to belong: being positively attached to other people

2   The need for power: influencing the goals and actions of others

3   The need for success: the enhancement of self-worth through achieving socially valued goals.

When these three needs coexist in a positive way then pupils will be ideal learners. Learners can enjoy belonging to their class, value the projects they are working on and enjoy the success of achieving set goals. These emotional needs are instrumental in driving pupils' behaviour and lead them to take up those roles within the group that help them meet their needs (see Figure 1).

EMOTIONAL NEED	BEHAVIOUR	ROLE WITHIN GROUP
approval	disruptive	class clown
care	passive	class mascot

FIGURE 1. Group roles

Awareness of these driving needs helps us to appreciate why we can only ever understand a child's behaviour if we look at the social context in which it takes place. To look at the child in isolation is to look at only half the answer. A pupil's behaviour is seeking to meet an emotional need within a group context. This leads us on to the third key question.

Why do so many children find it difficult to behave appropriately within class?

This is not a simple question – classroom behaviour is very complex and there are many interrelating factors that need to be understood to make sense of it. (If we fully understood it, then managing challenging behaviour in our classrooms would not be the problem that it clearly is in most schools.)

Some key factors

Ideally, before they even start attending school, most children will learn a number of social skills at home within the family group that match school expectations:

- how to behave as a group member
- how to gain attention
- which emotions it is OK to express
- how to resolve conflicts in socially acceptable ways
- how to negotiate and compromise.

Some of us may remember when schools used 'traditional' methods for teaching – pupils sat in rows of desks and the teacher was at the front imparting knowledge. In those days everything was much calmer than it is today. Many factors contributed to this, including:

- learners were expected to be more passive recipients of knowledge, therefore there were less interactions between learners and teacher
- teachers were perceived as being in charge and had higher status
- children and parents were socialised to accept unquestioningly what schools did
- education was valued as a means of offering work opportunities, therefore parents were supportive of its importance.

As schools have moved towards more co-operative and collaborative learning methods, however, more and more children face difficulties and exhibit challenging behaviour. Davinder, for example, finds doing project work with his classmates very difficult. He becomes frustrated when they give him tasks to do that he doesn't like and fails to understand why he should listen to the ideas of others who at times don't agree with his suggestions.

Why is this? A plausible explanation is that children enter school with fewer of the basic social skills necessary to engage in active learning. The changing pattern of children's games and the growing use of the media and computer games naturally reduce the opportunities for some children to learn social skills.

For those children whose home background helps develop such skills as listening and sharing, then school life is an extension of their family life and they are more likely to have the will to succeed. These children are used to listening to the ideas of others and then having their views asked for and respected. They have come to expect people to justify their views, as well as being prepared to compromise when differences occur. Such experiences are invaluable for today's classrooms.

If a child has some degree of learning difficulty this will compound his or her lack of social skills. In many schools, especially secondary schools, children who find learning difficult have turned the school culture and ethos on its head. They have made failure seem like success and they name-call those children who engage positively with school ('boffins' and 'swots'). It is understandable that children who expect to fail will seek to protect their self-esteem. To this end the social, emotional and behavioural difficulties that many children show in certain lessons and with specific adults can be seen as an attempt by the child to avoid failure.

For some children who enter school with low self-esteem and poor learning experiences, groups, particularly classroom groups, are extremely threatening places. The goals that adults set up for the group are goals that they realise they cannot succeed in, such as being expected to plan work together, to take on different roles and to defer immediate satisfaction of what they would like to do. If they could have some success within the group they would achieve a sense of personal power. It would also mean that they were pursuing goals set down by school, which would help to give them a sense of belonging to a community with shared values. Because of their low expectation to succeed many children develop alternative goals such as:

- to challenge adult authority
- to undermine the curriculum aims.

Developmental factors

In younger children a sense of personal identity is influenced and shaped by such key people as parents and school staff. The younger the children are the more they see themselves 'through the eyes of significant others'. They are more concerned about how adults, rather than their peers, think and feel about them. But as they grow older it is their peers who take on an increasingly important role. During adolescence it is the reactions of their peers that come to matter as much, and often more, than those of adults. The influence that parents have diminishes. This can help explain why it is in secondary schools that classroom behaviour becomes such an issue. Adolescents are placed in groups – usually with peers of both gender. The values and attitudes of the group now influence the behaviour of individuals. Being challenging towards adults can increase a young person's status within the group. The adult may punish the adolescent but the perception of the individual and the group is that he or she is asserting his or her autonomy.

2 Theory to practice – mistaken goal analysis

The question now is how we can use our awareness of group behaviour to help us understand and support those children who find it difficult to participate positively in class. If we agree that the emotional needs of children are the main drive for inappropriate behaviour we can begin to develop models that can help us intervene in a more focused manner.

Group roles

If pupils misbehave, either through excessive disruptive behaviour or through hurting another child, then they should face the consequences. However, if they belong to the minority who do not respond to negative consequences (punishments), this suggests that their behaviour is being maintained by other factors, that is internal needs that they have learned to fulfil in ways that are not acceptable in the classroom. Whereas most children learn through positive discipline how to get attention appropriately, some only receive negative attention and punishment now becomes 'positive feedback' as it is the only attention they receive.

The following model, called 'mistaken goal analysis', was developed by Dreikurs, Grunwald and Pepper (1998). It was based on the work of Alfred Adler (1957), a one-time follower of Freud who broke away. Adler believed that the main drive for all people is their need to belong. As most children with social, emotional and behavioural difficulties tend to act out (that is their difficulties are observable and are intended to have an impact on other people) more in a group context than when alone or in one-to-one situations, this model certainly seems to have some face validity for an understanding of the behaviour problems that arise in group contexts.

Mistaken goal analysis

Dreikurs et al. (1998) set out the four main goals, one or more of which seem to be found in children who present behaviour problems in the classroom. These are:

- attention
- power
- revenge
- nurture.

Most children develop positive ways of belonging to the group/class through making friends, sharing and co-operating. By 'mistaken goals' Dreikurs et al. suggest that some children develop unconscious goals that reflect their own real or imagined experiences, determining how they behave when in a group.

Attention

Children who fail to obtain a valued place in the group can come to strive for attention at any cost. Consequently, even though the attention they receive may be negative – for example the teacher feels annoyed at the child for shouting out and sanctions him – this is negative attention which satisfies the child's need for some form of attention. The child may show off with peers and receive negative feedback – for example not being chosen to join in. While the child's behaviour is not satisfying his need to belong, he is nonetheless trying to relate to both adults and his peers.

Power

The child who strives for power is confrontational and determined to win at any cost. Adults who take the child on find that she will always come back with some attempt to dominate. Karen, for example, has been told to return to her seat by her teacher. As she does so she mutters a negative comment which is barely audible but loud enough for the teacher to ask her what she has said. Karen replies, 'Nothing that concerns you.' Such children often suffer from a sense of inferiority, perhaps because their own views and attempts to control events in their lives have been over-dominated by others stronger than them, and this pushes them on to more and more extreme ways to 'get their own way'.

Revenge

Some children develop a strong sense of injustice and can believe that they have been hurt or wronged in some way. These children will behave in hurtful and spiteful ways towards both other children and adults, for example by spoiling a friend's work or using obscene language that they detect upsets the adults. It is as if they are saying, 'I've been hurt, so you feel some of the pain that I've felt.' Children who hurt others are usually hurting inside themselves.

Nurture

The child who seeks nurture is the typically passive child. Such children can feel that the challenges in the classroom are beyond them and they try to draw adults in to parent them. Tim, for example, will sit and sulk when given a new task and wait for an assistant to offer him help. These children are rarely disruptive to others, but find it hard to engage with new challenges.

This model asks us to see children's behaviour as another form of communication which is telling us something about their needs. The trouble is usually that busy adults take the behaviour at its surface level. If we look behind it we can find clues to what the child really needs and this can inform any support programme we wish to put in place.

Figure 2 is a problem-solving model. Before we can decide which interventions to put in place, we need to generate a 'plausible hypothesis' about which of the mistaken goals we think the child is pursuing within the group context.

STEP 1	Describe the behaviour fully and clearly as you see it. Make sure that your descriptions are objective. The term 'aggressive behaviour' could be interpreted in different ways, but describing how one pupil hit another on the shoulder is clear and observable.
STEP 2	Personal reflex – record how the child's behaviour typically makes you feel (see Figure 3).
STEP 3	Response reflex – record how the child usually responds to your attempts to reprimand him (see Figure 3).
STEP 4	Recognition reflex – when you put your idea to the child (in a caring way) as to why he behaves as he does, do you notice any tell-tale nonverbal responses (eyes look away, blushing, fidgeting, etc.) (see Figure 3)?
STEP 5	Choose interventions to respond to the child's behaviour in a way which will help the child to get his needs met more appropriately (see Figure 4).

FIGURE 2. Data collection

Having obtained a plausible hypothesis as to what the child's behaviour is achieving for him or her, Figure 4 suggests interventions which will help to:

- redirect the behaviour in a positive direction
- teach the child how to get his or her needs met in more appropriate ways.

PERSONAL REFLEX

ATTENTION	POWER	REVENGE	NURTURE
annoyed	angry	hurt	frustrated
resentful	threatened	dislike	concerned
coaxes	defeated	pity	caring
spends time	critical	sad	protective

RESPONSE REFLEX

ATTENTION
Student's response to being corrected:
stops and starts again

POWER
Student's response to being corrected:
continues, at an increased intensity

REVENGE
Student's response to being corrected:
angry and abusive, feels treated unfairly

NURTURE
Student's response to being corrected:
passive acceptance

RECOGNITION REFLEX

ATTENTION
COULD IT BE THAT:
You want to make me notice you?
You want me to help you more?
You want to be special?

POWER
COULD IT BE THAT:
You want to be in charge?
You want to show me I can't stop you?
You want to argue with me?

REVENGE
COULD IT BE THAT:
You have been hurt and want to hurt others?
You want to get even?
You want to argue with me?

NURTURE
COULD IT BE THAT:
You are afraid to try?
You want help at all times?
You want someone to care for you?

FIGURE 3. The three reflexes

Mistaken goal: plausible hypothesis	How to redirect student
POWER pupil is defiant and confrontational	• give responsibility/tasks • develop areas of strength • teach impulse-control skills • practise carrying out requests
REVENGE pupil often hurts or spoils work	• enhance self-esteem • set safety boundaries • develop empathy skills • teach ways of expressing feelings
NURTURE pupil is dependent on others	• promote independence • practise positive thinking • give choices • value contribution
ATTENTION pupil seeks adult time	• give attention when appropriate • use payback scheme • sit with role model • value contributions

FIGURE 4. Interventions for mistaken goals

There are many other plausible explanations for behavioural difficulties in learners. Below is a list of useful questions that can help us to decide which explanation to pursue, including the goals we have already considered.

Indicative questions

1 Does the behaviour occur when new learning tasks are set?
 YES: plausible hypothesis – learning difficulties.

2 Does the behaviour occur during free and unstructured times?
 YES: plausible hypothesis – poor social skills.

3 Is the behaviour confrontational towards adults?
 YES: plausible hypothesis – need for power.

4 Is the behaviour annoying towards adults?
 YES: plausible hypothesis – attention seeking.

5 Is the behaviour hurtful towards adults or other pupils?
 YES: plausible hypothesis – revenge.

6 Is the behaviour passive and dependent?
 YES: plausible hypothesis – need for nurture.

7 Has the child experienced any recent traumas?
 YES: plausible hypothesis – stress.

8 Does the pupil avoid mixing with peers?
 YES: plausible hypothesis – bullying/friendship difficulties.

9 Does the pupil respond negatively to specific adults?
 YES: plausible hypothesis – personality clash.

10 Has the pupil recently experienced loss or separation?
 YES: plausible hypothesis – bereavement.

Group behaviour

This problem-solving model can also help us understand the different roles that pupils take on in class. We are all familiar with such characters as: the bully, who dominates and forces his will on others; the class clown, who turns situations into being funny and entertaining to obtain attention; the victim, who seems to provoke others to treat her negatively; the leader, who has high status and helps the group achieve valued goals, for example in sport; and the class mascot, who is liked and protected by others and often is or acts younger than his peers and therefore needs some form of protection. It is reasonable to expect that the roles that children take up within a group reflect their internal emotional needs.

Using Figure 5 it is possible to see which roles dominate for any particular child. The typical behaviours that are associated with particular needs are grouped with those roles that usually enable these mistaken needs to be obtained. If you use such a grid for any particular pupil you will find that, while you do place some ticks everywhere, there will be a preponderance of ticks around a particular need. This will enable you either to discuss this with the pupil or to implement an intervention plan based on your analysis. To use the grid focus on the behaviours that you observe in a student and then see which role best fits the description

Classroom subgroups

Managing a large class is no easy achievement and doing so successfully demonstrates the true skill of the teacher. Trying to understand and meet the needs of 30 pupils would test anyone. A useful approach is to break the class down into subgroups, each of which have different needs to the others. There are two such models worth considering.

Model 1   The OK groups

Peter Galvin (1999) suggests that there are four main subgroups in a difficult-to-manage class. In Figure 6 you can see each of these subgroups identified and the key task for any classroom manager.

ROLE

BEHAVIOUR

Behaviour	POWER				BELONGING				GOALS			
	challenger	dominator	defier	bully	comedian	victim/loner	mascot	attention seeker	rebel	cynic	saboteur	loser
Refuses requests												
Answers back												
Verbally aggressive												
Physically aggressive												
Has few friends												
Fools around												
Follows the crowd												
Petty interruptions												
Lacks motivation												
Disaffected												
Avoids new challenges												
No homework/equipment												

FIGURE 5. Functional analysis of behaviour and roles

Subgroup 1. The very OK
The top five. These are the pupils who nearly always behave well. Because of this they are often passed over. They need feedback, an occasional but regular good word about how much they are valued.

Subgroup 2. The average OK
Around 15. These are the pupils who are little trouble, the 'run-of-the-mill' kids as Galvin refers to them. They will finish their school career with, 'Thanks, I'm off'. They need to be motivated and involved.

Subgroup 3. The not very OK
About eight. These are the pupils that we cannot ignore. They are constantly needing guidance, reminders, reprimands and sanctions and seem to thrive on disrupting any lesson. They have to be managed.

Subgroup 4. The desperately not OK
Around two. These are the pupils who are either statemented for their special needs or you wish they were. They usually display difficult behaviours in a wide range of different contexts, both structured and unstructured. You are usually aware of their background and they are pupils who have probably faced a number of out-of-school at-risk factors.

FIGURE 6. Model 1 – the OK groups

If you are faced with a difficult class Galvin suggests that the subgroup that will pay immediate dividends is subgroup 3. These are the students you cannot ignore, therefore the sooner you get to know them the more effective your management strategies can be.

Model 2   Motivation, expectancy and effort

The effort that pupils make in any lesson can be summed up by the following equation:

$$\text{effort} = f\,(\text{expectancy/value})$$

That is to say, effort depends on pupils' expectations to succeed and the value they place on what they are learning. This model can help us break a class down into four subgroups. See Figure 7.

Subgroup A. The engaged
Pupils who expect to succeed and value the curriculum are our ideal pupils. They engage willingly in our lessons.

Subgroup B. The avoiders
Pupils who know they could manage the work, but don't see the point or the value of it, will do as little as possible.

Subgroup C. Those needing protection
Pupils who value the work you set them but do not believe they can cope with it will seek to protect their fragile self-esteem. These are the pupils who answer 'yes' when you ask if they have understood your instructions. You might know that they will not be able to do the work without some form of support.

Subgroup D. The rejectors
These are the pupils who are at risk of truanting. They neither value the curriculum nor have any expectation to succeed if they tried.

FIGURE 7. Model 2 – motivation, expectancy and effort

By looking at a class through model 2 you can see that the different behaviours you observe can be explained in different terms. Each group will benefit from focused support as they each have different reasons for not working in the class.

Some ideas as to how we might support each of the subgroups in model 2 are presented in Figure 8.

Subgroup A. The engaged
As this group is engaged there is no need for interventions.

Subgroup B. The avoiders
- involve interests – can their hobbies and interests be used in their learning?
- cost–benefit analysis – what will be the students' gains for trying harder?
- analyse long-term goals – do the students have long-term goals that can be related to their present situation?
- alternative curriculum – are there any alternative, work-related courses that they could join?

Subgroup C. Those needing protection
- learning support – is there a learning mentor available to work with them?
- record successes – can their short-term successes be highlighted?
- differentiate learning goals – make sure targets set match their current abilities
- small group work – can they work with supportive peers?

Subgroup D. The rejectors
- home–school links – actively contact and involve parents/carers
- counselling – make one-to-one time available to explore issues
- goal-setting – involve students in setting realistic goals
- combine strategies for subgroups B and C that are appropriate (this is because all behaviour has a mixture of different motives and is rarely explained simply by one factor).

FIGURE 8. Interventions for model 2

When you use either of these models be sure to write the actual names of the pupils under each heading. This can be used as a reminder to you as to the type of intervention that is most likely to be effective with each student or group.

3 Group skills

The 'problem' behaviour in class of many children is a reflection of their lack of the core skills needed to function successfully in today's classrooms. The increased emphasis on learning in groups, of learning being a social activity, is a huge change from traditional methods. More and more schools are recognising that some children misbehave not because they are unwilling to conform but because they are unable to conform. They lack the core skills. And when this combines with low expectations to succeed through a history of learning difficulties then it is hardly surprising that their frustrations lead them to behave inappropriately. Using the core group skills profile presented below you will be able to see where the areas of weakness are for a particular pupil.

A score of three or less in any category indicates that this is an area for development. Above three shows a functional level of competency.

If a pupil lacks those core skills that are essential for successful group work then positive action needs to be taken to ensure positive progress. Even the most effective sanction will not teach a pupil how to do what she currently cannot do.

Scaffolding

A helpful term when constructing an individual support programme is 'scaffolding'. For Vygotsky (1962) learning is a social process. Children learn from those they interact with – peers and adults. Scaffolding is the process by which the next step in the learning process is modelled or cued. The process of scaffolding also occurs with behaviour. Children who have not experienced adults modelling trust, care, listening, etc. sufficiently for them to have learnt these social skills will require

Core group skills profile

Student's name:..

Completed by: ....

Date:..

Circle the number in the one column which best describes the student.

		Rarely	Sometimes	Often	Always
Social Competence					
1	Gets on well with peers	0	1	2	3
2	Mixes appropriately with strangers	0	1	2	3
3	Can express needs to range of adults	0	1	2	3
4	Behaves well in school	0	1	2	3
5	Relates well with other family members	0	1	2	3

SCORE   /15

		Rarely	Sometimes	Often	Always
Personal Interaction Skills					
6	Uses eye contact appropriately	0	1	2	3
7	Contributes to conversations	0	1	2	3
8	Aware of verbal and nonverbal cues	0	1	2	3
9	Can empathise with others	0	1	2	3
10	Can give and accept compliments	0	1	2	3

SCORE   /15

		Rarely	Sometimes	Often	Always
Social Problem-solving					
11	Deals with unfair criticism	0	1	2	3
12	Can think of a range of solutions	0	1	2	3
13	Can make new friends	0	1	2	3
14	Manages conflicts positively	0	1	2	3
15	Deals with teasing effectively	0	1	2	3

SCORE   /15

scaffolding to enable them to move from their existing limited skills to new skills appropriate for success in group work.

Imran

Imran (eight years old) seemed able to cope when in a small group of two or three. At such times he seemed to relate well with his peers, sharing toys and being generally co-operative. However, during playtimes when there were many more children around he seemed to forget all these skills. He would run around the playground bumping into other children and seemed unable to play organised games such as football.

Scaffolding techniques

1   Observation. With an adult, Imran observed the games other children were playing and discussed what was happening.

2   Role differentiation. Using role play, Imran played games which involved him behaving differently in different situations.

3   Buddying. Several other children were involved in supporting Imran for short periods of playtimes, during which Imran was actively encouraged to take part in a football game – sometimes being the goalkeeper, sometimes striker.

Outcome

After a four-week period Imran was securely involved in the organised games during playtimes and was a lot more confident in himself

---

Scaffolding principle

In devising a programme to help students develop the necessary social skills we need to analyse their current skill levels in a specific context. To achieve this the following questions need to be considered.

1   What can they do now?

2   What can they do with support?

3   What do I need to do to help them?

4 Managing difficult groups

'The elephant in the kitchen' syndrome

When we are confronted by difficult or unpleasant situations there is a normal tendency in all of us to avoid truths that can be painful. Imagine a family which has a huge elephant in the kitchen. Everybody squeezes around it, but no one will ask the question, 'What is that elephant doing in the kitchen?' for fear of breaking the family secret. This can be the same with difficult groups – the painful truth is avoided. Jasmine, for example, is being bullied by a number of girls in her class. All the other members of the class know that this is going on, but no one will talk about it. Her class teacher is aware that things are not right but doesn't know why. The shock tactic of bringing the secret into the open, however, can often be the first step in going forward. Children, like adults, are used to looking the other way. Show your determination to improve relationships, teaching and learning.

Below are some principles and techniques worth bearing in mind when you are dealing with a difficult group.

1   Stranger in the room. Visitors can create new dynamics that can positively affect pupils' behaviour. You might, for example, invite into the classroom a colleague, a parent or students from another class doing some observations.

2   Shock tactics. Put aside your lesson plan and, in a caring way, challenge the group to look at the difficulties that are preventing you teaching and them learning.

3   Self-esteem activities. Develop a wide range of ways to show that there are positive consequences for appropriate behaviour. Such rewards could be a special video, visit or a student-chosen activity.

4   Letters home for positive reasons. Be ready to send notes home commenting on improvements, contributions, effort, etc. Pupils in difficult groups need encouragement to risk changing.

General guidelines

Always treat difficult groups with respect and avoid talking down to them. Show through your behaviour that you are determined to be consistent and fair.

The quicker you can establish routines the better it will be. Spend time establishing how students come into your room, how equipment is distributed, how homework is set and collected and how latecomers are dealt with. If getting specific equipment ready disrupts your teaching, establish a routine to deal with it.

You can have the greatest impact when you begin to teach a new group. The students probably don't yet know each other and this is when you can establish your expectations. If you do not a group culture will develop, which might be negative.

Rewards, responsibilities and self-esteem

Keep a log book of students' good behaviour, achievements, etc. At the end of each week read out their successes. Your intention is to break any well-established routines of members of the group defining themselves through their problem behaviour.

Have a reward system so that you can quickly and quietly give positive feedback on behaviour or work that you like (for example sticky dots). Reward students when they have completed even simple jobs. Set lots of easy (but realistic) tasks to ensure success. Send pupils to other members of staff to show their work.

Make a point of turning problem behaviours into ways of increasing students' personal responsibility. Make sure that they understand that it is their behaviour that determines either the rewards or punishments that they receive. They are responsible for their behaviour and your intention should be to help them take this responsibility and make the best choices.

Rules, routines and sanctions

Always start lessons in a set, organised way. Make sure you give your attention to those who are carrying out your instructions appropriately.

The more that pupils are involved in making the rules then the easier it will be for you to enforce them on their behalf. If you establish that they each have a right to learn, that others have the same right and that you have the right to teach then any disruption can be dealt with now as violating a basic ground rule of the group.

React quietly to any individual who is causing disruption. Remind her of your expectation and leave her with a 'Return to your seat, thank you'. This conveys an expectation that the individual will carry out your request. Remember that many adolescents, especially, view 'hard requests' as threats to their freedom (a core aspiration) and respond with increased defiance. 'Return to your seat' can be seen as an open invitation to a power struggle and a defiant response of 'make me'. While 'Return to your seat, thank you', with the adult turning away from the student, allows the student to do as asked but when she is ready, thus 'saving face'.

Don't make an issue out of low-level disruption but make sure the pupils know your procedure for dealing with challenging behaviour. Increase the sanction if the pupil begins to disrupt others or you.

Always follow through on sanctions. To the pupil it is the certainty that something will happen rather than the size of the consequence that is effective.

Grouping

Be decisive about seating in your room and change seating regularly. When you allow students to sit with friends make sure it is conditional upon them working effectively.

Encourage students to co-operate with each other by using team points in the form of marks out of ten for group work, to be given to the group as a whole. At the end of the week allocate rewards negotiated with the class, such as choosing activities, if teams have earned at least 50% of their potential score.

Activities, tasks and targets

Use short, timed tasks to build up to more detailed or difficult work. Breaking projects down ensures that at the end of a lesson each pupil can have a sense of achievement. One way to do this is to set five different tasks on different tables. Individuals or groups do as much as they can in ten minutes and then move on.

> *Remember:* set (short) task, give feedback, set task, give feedback, etc.

5 The group leader

Whether you are the leader of the class or of a small group it is you who are in charge. Knowledge of the group will also allow you to spot the leaders within groups. Working with these leaders will have a ripple effect, in that if you influence such key people in the group they will influence others who look to them for approval. Remember that young people look to their peers as their key reference group – we should make use of this knowledge.

Your aim is to remove those barriers that prevent children engaging with the learning experience that you have planned for them. We have seen that there are many reasons why some children try to avoid engaging with work in groups. It is, therefore, all the more important when a group is being established that you ensure that the correct group norms are stressed. It might be that you take some key norms from your school's behaviour policy. For example these might be:

- the right to learn
- the right to be safe
- the right to be valued.

These could be used as a starting point. You can then discuss what these mean within your class or group. Frequent reminders of these rules will be essential for those groups whose behaviour can be challenging. By adding some rules that are unique to your group you will encourage a sense of belonging, identity and ownership.

Remember that when your group has established their rights they need also to consider their responsibilities, namely:

- to enable others to learn
- to help others to feel safe
- to value others
- to respect the opinions of others.

Developing group identity

Helping a class develop a sense of belonging is a very important process. The pupils we are talking about here are each struggling, sometimes fighting, for a position in the group. While a classroom is not the jungle (it just feels like that sometimes) we should not ignore some basic principles of group psychology. Classrooms cause tensions – the need to be an individual versus the need to be a group member.

You might like to try the following activity on your pupils – and yourself. Ask students if they can write down ten different answers to the question:

'Who am I?'

If you collect in their answers you will find that some fall under one or other of these two headings:

1 *Collectivistic qualities* – the answer shows the student's awareness of self in relationship to others, e.g. 'I am a student', 'I am a boy/girl'.

2 *Individualistic qualities* – the answer reflects personal traits, habits or interests, e.g. 'I am a football fan', 'I am a happy person'.

Is your group made up of individuals who define themselves more in collectivistic terms or individualistic terms? While there are no right or wrong answers the traits that each individual brings can make a group identity easier or harder to achieve. If there is a predominance of individualistic traits within the group then there is a definite need to develop some collectivistic qualities to avoid the group being over-competitive:

Individualistic	Collectivistic
personal goals	shared goals
competitive	co-operative

The more positive an identity pupils can have towards their group then the more confident and positive they will be towards the tasks set them. Ideally each pupil would:

- value his/her own contribution to the group
- be proud to be part of the group
- believe that others rate the group positively.

Achieving group identity – some ideas

1   Develop group structure, that is have a range of classroom responsibilities that all members must at some time fulfil, for example taking on the role of paper/display board monitor.

2   Give feedback to the group from other high-status individuals, such as the head or a deputy head teacher, as to how much progress they are seen to be making.

3   Give feedback on results of group effort, such as by displaying work in class or around school.

4   Set targets and rewards that can be achieved only through each member contributing within the group, for example, someone records a project, another produces models and a third makes a quiz or word search to use when the project is being presented to others.

5   Develop routines and rituals for recognising group success, for example the theme song of the local football team could be played on special occasions.

6   Develop a group record that allows individuals to record successes. This should include objective, methods used, date complete and comments on the outcome.

7   Make a photographic record of the group's activities, either to be kept in a file or displayed on the class wall.

8   Develop a routine for saying goodbye to any class members when they leave, for whatever reason, for example with a card completed by all members of the group, and ways of welcoming new members, such as sharing group experiences and memories and pairing the new member up with a buddy.

9   Develop a class motto, for example by putting the group's own words to the theme song of the local football team.

10   Join with the group in extracurricular activities such as sport or music.

Remember the norm of reciprocity – 'you get what you give'. The more positive and determined you are for the group to succeed the more likely you are to receive help from them in your goal. Aggressive and punitive control techniques, such as shouting and using threats, produce the same responses (aggressive behaviours and a non-co-operative attitude) in students.

Leaders' qualities, skills and attitude

There are many personal qualities and skills that combine to make a leader either effective or not. The four key behavioural techniques that require further consideration are as follows:

1   Nonverbal behaviour.

2   Creating a plan of action – trial and error learning.

3   Accentuating the positive.

4   Personal resiliency.

A complex system will only change when individuals are prepared to tackle the problems they face. When you become aware of a problem with a group it becomes an opportunity for you to improve the group. If you ignore it, it will not get better. Children with social, emotional and behavioural difficulties have more respect for school staff who try to improve matters than those who just accept them.

1. Nonverbal behaviour

While we may be conscious of the content of what we are saying, the real impact comes from the way we say it. Being mindful of our body language can help us project a confident and assertive message when managing groups of children. Voice control is also an aspect of nonverbal communication. We can convey enthusiasm, determination and concern by the slightest change in voice tone.

2. Plan of action

Use the framework below to set up a mini project systematically.

Step 1 – identify and describe
What is the problem?

- Students arrive at the lesson in dribs and drabs and fool around until I shout and demand quiet.

Step 2 – data collection
How often does it occur, where, when and with whom?

- It happens at the beginning of the two lessons I take them for each week. It takes around ten minutes before I can start the work for that lesson.

Step 3 – plausible hypothesis
Why do you think it is like this?

- They see little relevance in learning French.

Step 4 – action plan
What could be done?

i   I could have some games, word searches or quizzes already set out for them to start as soon as they enter the class.

ii   I could give responsibilities such as handing out books, etc. to those who seem most disruptive.

iii   I could send notes home whenever the class made good progress.

iv   I could remind them of the class rules to arrive punctually and settle quickly.

v   I could see them all at the end of the day to make up for lost work.

Proactive techniques, i.e. to prevent it happening – i, ii and iii.
Reactive techniques, i.e. after it has happened – iv and v.

Step 5 – review

Remember: with a plan of action you are being proactive and

being proactive = control = personal confidence.

3. Accentuate the positive

Any group that is presenting a wide range of behavioural difficulties can lead adults into the negativity trap, that is that when reasoning doesn't work we shout, and when shouting doesn't work we resort to threats of detention, then if that doesn't work we threaten removal from the class. We gradually increase the punishment, believing that at some point our students will respond and do as we wish. In actual fact they are probably thriving on negative attention as well as believing that they are winning by preventing us from teaching. This is where relationships between pupils and adults are now soured. Feedback tends to be negative and everyone, teacher and pupils alike, is glad when the lesson is over. Below is a list of questions that will help you keep certain principles at the front of your mind.

1 Have you used a variety of reward systems (verbal rewards, tangible activities)?

2 Have you set clear, obtainable learning targets for the group?

3 Did you begin the lesson by highlighting progress to date?

4 Are you using a whole-class reward system?

5 Did you send any student to senior management for praise?

6 Have you sent any commendation letters or phoned home with good news?

7 Did the group help you decide the class rules?

8 Have you reminded the class of their rules?

9 Do you focus on those behaving appropriately first?

10 Are you recording signs of improvements?

4. Personal resiliency

If we look at the behaviour from a distance, a 'bird's eye view', we can discern patterns and triggers. We can look for what happened before the behaviour and what followed it. We can look for those variables that we have some influence over, for example seating arrangements and the amount of positive feedback that we give to a group. It is through increasing our understanding of behaviour that we increase our resiliency to the negative effects that challenging and disruptive behaviour can have.

Some basic facts about behaviour

- Children are trying to solve a problem – not to be one.
- Behaviour always has a purpose.
- Good behaviour can be learned just as bad behaviour can.
- Resistance to change is normal.
- Children's behaviour often gets worse before it gets better.
- Change is gradual – but inevitable.

- Accentuate the positive – eliminate the negative.
- It is the behaviour that is the problem, not the child.
- Children with emotional, behavioural and social difficulties need advocates. If not you, who? If not now, when?

And finally some survival tips...

1   Stay calm and controlled.

2   Avoid letting your own behaviour make matters worse by, for example, becoming aggressive.

3   Prioritise. Work on one aspect – for example how you finish a lesson – not everything at once.

4   Develop techniques based on priorities.

5   Look at the situation from the student's point of view.

6   Assess any changes in the student's behaviour or work output – and keep assessing.

7   Use pre-prepared ways to help you think and act, for example count to ten and ask the student what it is that he or she should be doing.

8   Work as a team – talk with colleagues.

Further reading

References

Adler, A. (1957) *Understanding Human Behaviour*. New York: Fawcett.

Dreikurs, R., Grunwald, B. and Pepper, F. (1998) *Maintaining Sanity in the Classroom*. London: Accelerated Development.

Galvin, P. (1999) *Behaviour and Discipline in Schools: practical, positive and creative strategies for the classroom*. London: David Fulton Publishers.

Vygotsky, L. (1962) *Thought and Language*. Massachusetts: The M.I.T. Press.

Recommended reading

Corrie, L. (2002) *Investigating troublesome classroom behaviour: practical tools for teachers*. London: Routledge Falmer.

Forsyth, D. (1999) *Group Dynamics*. Belmont, CA: Brooks/Cole.